GEORGE MEADE'S
NEW YORK

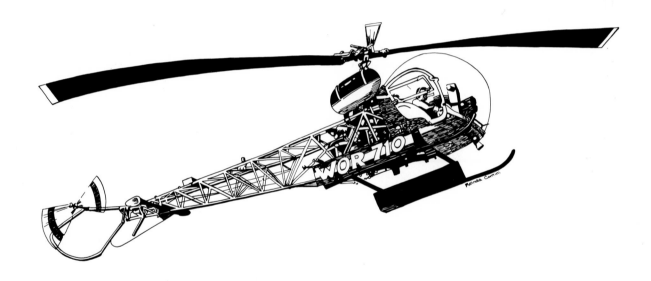

PHOTOGRAPHY BY KIP COLLIGAN

An Original ATLANTIC FLYWAY, INCORPORATED Book.

GEORGE MEADE'S NEW YORK

Library of Congress Catalogue No. 80-67817
Copyright prints of color plates in this volume are available
from Atlantic Flyway, Inc. [See Print Information at end of book.]

PRINTING HISTORY:
First U.S. Edition: September 1980
Second U.S. Edition: February 1981

Printed in the United States of America by Regensteiner Press.
Distributed in the U.S.A. by Random House, Inc.
and in Canada by Random House of Canada, Ltd.

ISBN 394-74831-X soft-cover
ISBN 394-51786-5 hard-cover

Designed by **KIPANY** *Productions*

Editor: Tiffany Hendry
Art Director: Melinda Contini
Design Assistant: Thomas Jenkins

CONTENTS

FOREWORD

Welcome to *George Meade's New York*—and share his unique view of the most exciting city in the world.

Five mornings each week, George lifts Helicopter 710 off the pad at Teterboro Airport in New Jersey, and flies across the Hudson River to meet his tall friends in Manhattan...Citicorp, Empire State, World Trade, and Chrysler. He takes a three hour flight to nowhere, keeping New York commuters alert to the ever-changing pattern of cars and trucks struggling into the City.

And in his 7,000 hours of flying over New York, George has collected the most beautiful and unusual photographs ever taken of The Big Apple.

There are many days when I envy George... his front row seat on a spectacular Long Island sunrise...the sun setting behind the Statue of Liberty...or the City's nighttime sparkle. But there are other times when gusty March winds bounce his little helicopter around like a toy...when spring fog and rain reduce visibility to a frightening few yards...when lightning and thunderheads etch that famous skyline...that's when I'm very glad not to be in George's flight boots.

But for 12 years, George's unflappable good humor and uncanny ability to report traffic problems quickly and clearly have been an important part of "Rambling with Gambling" on WOR radio. George never flies without a camera, but for the most dramatic pictures of the big town he calls on Kip Colligan to fly shotgun on many of 710's daily traffic patrols. This airborne team, experienced pilot and creative photographer, have recorded views of the city that are spectacular.

So fasten your seat belt, hang on while George cranks up Helicopter 710, and come flying over George Meade's New York.

John Gambling

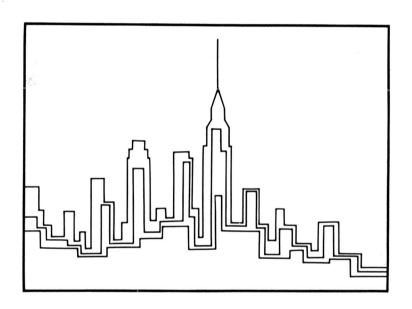

THE CITY

New York, New York...The Big Apple...latitude, 40° 42' 20"...longitude, 74° 0' 40"...the financial, cultural, and communications capital of the world...and home to nearly eight million people.

In Helicopter 710, a thousand feet above the traffic, noise and towering buildings, I fly over the most exciting and valuable piece of real estate in the world. From my perch I see 400,000 daily visitors come and go, and help 1.6 million commuters clogging the 6,000 miles of city streets and highways.

New York City has five boroughs. Each borough is also a county. And, the borough name is different from the county name...sometimes. But that's just one little quirk in this marvelous town. Staten Island claims the highest elevation, Queens is the most densely populated, Brooklyn has the most churches, the Bronx boasts one of the best zoos in the world, and when you go into Manhattan from any other borough, New Yorkers say you are going into "the City".

New York is Broadway and the theaters—the Empire State Building and The World Trade Center—the garment district and Fashion Avenue—the Bowery and Wall Street—Rockefeller Center and Harlem—the United Nations and Soho—East Side, West Side, Uptown, Downtown—with Central Park in the middle.

But words and statistics tell only part of New York's story. Pictures tell it best. *George Meade*

Citicorp points to the 80's.

Flying south at 1,000 feet over Central Park. The residential and business towers of Manhattan frame an oasis of green, broken only by the massive Metropolitan Museum of Art.

above: **The golden City, as seen by residents of Brooklyn Heights, one of the best views anywhere.**

opposite: **Looking west across Forty-Second Street the Chrysler and Empire State Buildings tower above their neighbors. The small structure to the left of the United Nations Building is actually a vent for the subway.**

15

THE WATERWAYS...

Of the City's five boroughs, only one, the Bronx, is *not* an island. Manhattan is separated from the mainland by the Hudson and Harlem rivers, and Staten Island has the Kill Van Kull on its New Jersey shore. Queens and Brooklyn are part of Long Island, the largest coastal island in the United States.

New York's harbor is the finest natural port on the Eastern Seaboard. Indian canoes...Dutch trading sloops... British warships...fishing trawlers...tugboats...the first nuclear freighter ...luxury liners...pleasure craft...tall ships and small have plied the waterways off New York's 770 miles of shoreline.

My daily flight takes me along this network of waterways...the original source of New York's wealth and international prestige.

THE BRIDGES

People walk, jog, bike, and roller skate on them...cars, buses, trucks, and trains cross them...some people fish from them...and, I fly over and *under* some of the 65 bridges of New York.

The oldest is High Bridge, spanning the Harlem River since 1848. The newest bridge is one most New Yorkers never cross, the bridge to Rikers Island Prison erected in 1966.

The Verrazano-Narrows Bridge is the longest suspension bridge in the world—and the Lemon Creek Bridge on Staten Island, just 34 feet from end to end, is the shortest in the City. But no matter what age or size, bridges bring New Yorkers together.

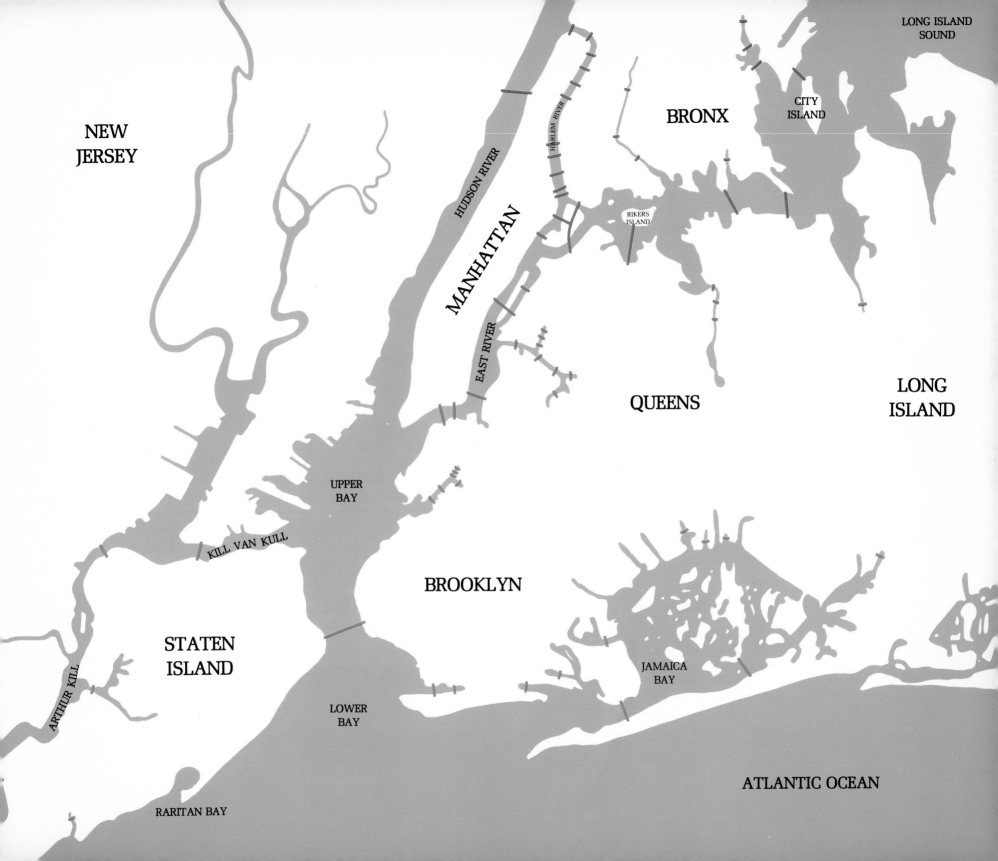

New Yorkers can use their waterways to get to work or to get away.

City Island is a quaint fishing village tucked away in the Bronx.

above: **Commuters stuck in bumper to bumper traffic on the East River Drive can at least watch the ships.**

opposite: **Dusk...and two Staten Island ferryboats glide across the lower bay like toys in a giant tub.**

above: **The New York City Marathon starts on the Verrazano-Narrows Bridge.**

opposite: **The towers and cables of the Whitestone and Throgs Neck Bridges weave an unusual web.**

Morning haze at the Triboro Bridge.

The Henry Hudson Bridge carries traffic over the Harlem River, with a lovely view of the majestic Hudson and the New Jersey Palisades.

Manhattan bound from New Jersey over the George Washington Bridge.

Looking north up the East River, the Harlem River, winds to the left and Hell Gate to the right. The little key shaped island (insert) was originally 2 islands called the Mill Rocks. In the early 1900's they were joined together to break up the strong currents.

Where once a tidal grist mill stood, a wind powered generator will soon be built.

above: **A supertanker in Brooklyn.**

opposite: **Before the George Washington Bridge was built, this little red lighthouse was used for navigation. Nestled under the eastern tower, it valiantly fights graffiti, vandalism, and the weather.**

above: **The stone towers of the Brooklyn Bridge were the tallest structures in the city when it was completed in 1883. The first of the East River crossings is still the most graceful.**

opposite: **The Manhattan Bridge at first light.**

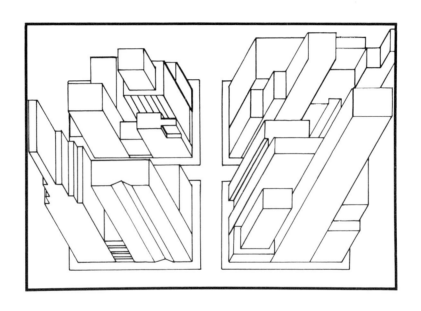

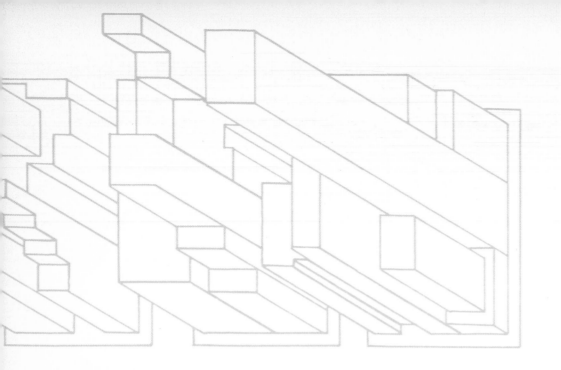

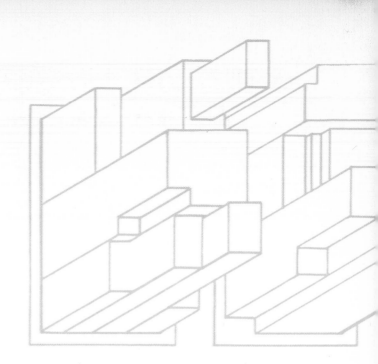

HIDDEN CITY

New York City boasts three of the four tallest buildings in the world. Yet, even from the top of the World Trade Center or the Empire State Building, you see only part of New York.

Look down into steel canyons and concrete valleys and find the hidden city, a source of never-ending surprises. These are the nooks and crannies of New York.

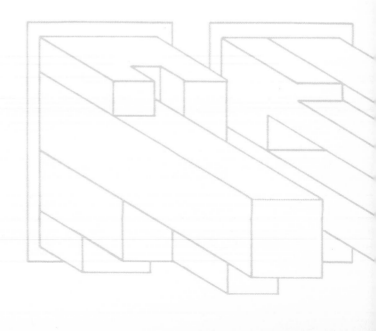

A bird's eye view of the House of Birds, at the Bronx Zoo...one of the City's architectural gems.

above: **Nine hundred young people board these venerable World War II ships to learn about the food and maritime industries. John Brown I & II may be the only floating high school in the country.**

opposite: **It looks like the famous Louisville Baseball bat. But it is actually the smokestack for the Yankee Stadium generator.**

left: **The Cathedral of St. John the Divine is the largest Gothic church in the world. Construction began in 1892, but it still remains unfinished.**

opposite: **The Delacorte Fountain, at the southern end of Roosevelt Island in the East River, sprays 4,000 gallons of water per minute 300 feet in the air.**

right: **The only authentic Chinese Pagoda in North America is part of the Institute for Asian studies at St. Johns University, in Queens.**

opposite: **This is Ellis Island, the gateway to the United States for 16 million immigrants. The Federal Government is creating a museum on the island.**

above: **The aerodynamic design of these three houses of worship are a clue of their location...J.F.K. International Airport.**

left: **From the air, this full size wrought iron model of a World War I fighter plane seems about to take off from the roof of 77 Water Street.**

43

above: **Fall at the Bronx Botanical Garden. This glass fairyland was recently refurbished.**

opposite: **Coney Island is Brooklyn's seaside amusement park, home of the Wonder Wheel and the Cyclone roller coaster.**

above: **This gracious home, built in 1806, was occupied by the Base Commander of the old New York Naval Shipyard.**

opposite: **On the Queen's side of the East River, Con Edison's Ravenswood Plant produces enough electricity to light up the entire state of Vermont.**

left: **Gracie Mansion, overlooking the East River at 88th Street, was built by a wealthy shipping merchant in 1799. It is the residence of the Mayor of New York.**

above: **Removing 34 million pounds of refuse from New York everday is an unending task. Sanitation trucks line up on the loading dock and await their turn to fill the barges that tugs push down the East River to a Staten Island land fill.**

opposite: **Paris? Rome? No...it's the Grand Army Plaza, hub of the fourth largest city in America, Brooklyn, New York...**

above: **Manhattan's last railroad yard, the Hudson River's ancient piers, and the crumbling West Side Highway all wait...**

opposite: **The United Nations is built on international soil. The slim tower by the river is the U.N. Secretariat building, only 72 feet wide. The Citicorp building has the slanted roof.**

above: **Forest Hills, in Queens, is one of New York's earliest planned communities. The winding streets and tudor architecture give it the atmosphere of a small English town.**

opposite: **The "Hall of Fame for Great Americans", it's not a hall at all, but a semi-circular colonade containing the busts of 95 famous Americans, located in the Bronx.**

53

MOODS

Each New York day has a special mood...a sunny spring morning, a cold winter sunrise...summer's heat and haze...and fall's crisp CAVU weather—"ceiling and visibility unlimited."

The City's clouds, rain, fog, and snow are often breathtaking and sometimes frightening.

When weather and stone and steel collide, a City of Moods appears.

Each one was the tallest in the world. Now the Chrysler and Empire State buildings blend into one with the setting October sun.

above: **The World Trade Center ...110 stories high...second tallest in the world...where 75,000 people come and go everyday...and 43,000 windows have to be washed.**

opposite: **A light dusting of snow adds sparkle to La Guardia Airport at dusk.**

Summer haze softens a lower
Manhattan morning. The view is
north from Governor's Island.

Sunrise breaks through lower Manhattan and onto the Hudson River.

The setting sun reflects on the stilled East River between Lower Manhattan and Brooklyn.

THE LADY

Her real name is "Liberty Enlightening the World."

Visitors climb 293 steps to her crown. Her fingers are longer than a man is tall. Her waist measures 35 feet across and she weighs 450,000 pounds.

The Statue of Liberty—New York's First Lady.

Not like the brazen giant of Greek fame,
With conquering limbs astride from land to land;

Here at our sea-washed, sunset gates shall stand
A mighty woman with a torch, whose flame
Is the imprisoned lightning, and her name
Mother of Exiles....

......From her beacon-hand
Glows world-wide welcome; her mild eyes command
The air-bridged harbor that twin cities frame.

"Keep ancient lands, your storied pomp!" cries she
With silent lips. "Give me your tired, your poor,
Your huddled masses yearning to breathe free.
The wretched refuse of your teeming shore.
Send these, the homeless, tempest-tost to me."

"I lift my lamp beside the golden door!"

—Sonnet by Emma Lazarus
engraved upon tablet within base of the
Statue of Liberty

MANHATTAN

1.

2.

3.

4.

5.

6.

7.

8.

9.

10.

THE TEN BEST PLACES TO PHOTOGRAPH
MANHATTAN

1. **FORT LEE PARK**, off Hudson Terrace, south of the George Washington Bridge. Spectacular vantage point for the Bridge and the Upper Westside, down to Midtown.
2. **ALEXANDER HAMILTON PLAZA**, a picture book view of midtown Manhattan to the east, and south to the World Trade Center. Bring change for the telescopes.
3. **HOBOKEN SHORE ROAD**, in back of Stevens Institute. Views of the Hudson River, Manhattan piers, midtown skyline, and the World Trade Center.
4. **MONTGOMERY STREET** opposite the World Trade Center, this site provides an awesome view of the Twin Towers. One block to the south on York Street there are park benches to sit on.
5. **LIBERTY STATE PARK**. off exit 14B on the New Jersey Turnpike Extension gives the photographer an insight on the Statue of Liberty's own view of lower Manhattan. To the south, Staten Island and the Verrazano-Narrows Bridge, to the northeast Ellis Island, the World Trade Center, and midtown Manhattan.
6. **WARDS ISLAND**, access from the Triborough Bridge and the 102nd Street footbridge affords southerly view of the East River, Gracie Mansion and the Eastside of Manhattan.
7. **ROOSEVELT ISLAND**, just a tramway ride away gives the photographer views of the 59th Street Bridge, midtown Manhattan and closeups of tugs and other assorted boats.
8. **FROM 14th DRIVE**, off Vernon Boulevard, midtown Manhattan, the United Nations, and the 59th Street Bridge are all in view.
9. **CADMAN PLAZA WEST** and Furman Street, beneath the Brooklyn Bridge, create an unusual view of river traffic, three bridges, lower Manhattan, and the South Street Seaport.
10. **COLUMBIA HEIGHTS** and Pineapple Street, the dock area frames the financial district, the Harbor, and Governors Island.

THE PHOTOGRAPHER

Kip Colligan's parents were very much involved with the performing arts. His mother Elsa, was an aerialist for *Ringling Brothers Barnum and Bailey Circus* and his father, James, was a television and film producer-director.
Kip studied film making at Hunter College in New York City and for several years worked as a cinematographer and film editor for television sports programs and industrial films.
In 1972, Kip became vice president of an established film and multi-media production company. Five years later, Kip with his wife and partner, Tiffany founded their own company, *Kipany Productions, Ltd.* They have created a variety of audio/visual programs for some of the world's largest corporate and governmental organizations. Kip's photographs have appeared in leading newspapers and magazines. His work has been singled out for numerous awards and citations.
Kip and Tiffany reside in Montclair, New Jersey and New York City, where Kip captains his boats: *Kipany* and *Kipany Too.*

THE FLIGHT

July 4th, 1976, America's birthday and New York City's "once in a life time" spectacular, *Operation Sail!* It was this celebration that brought Kip and George together...they quickly combined their talents to produce a series of audio/visual programs which have been seen by over 500,000 people.

THE PILOT

George Meade, a native New Yorker, learned his airborne skills in Seton Hall University's R.O.T.C flight program and then entered the United States Army. Here he flew over 1,000 combat missions in Vietnam, attaining the rank of captain and earning 26 medals. As WOR radio's helicopter-traffic reporter, George has broadcasted over 40,000 traffic reports. And in addition he has covered events around the City from the Pope's Visit to the Marathon. He has translated his flying experiences into several entertaining and informative slide presentations about his unusual job, which he shows to tens of thousands of people each year.

With 12 years of helicopter-traffic reporting behind him, George can still say, "It's satisfying and fascinating...I never dreamed of becoming a heliocopter pilot, or any kind of a pilot for that matter. Now, I can't imagine doing anything else!"

George lives in New Jersey with his wife Barbara, and their children, Tracy, Colleen, Heather and Michael.

Since then, George and Kip have worked together on many airborne photographic projects all over the Metropolitan area.

So next time you see WOR radio's helicopter overhead, look up and smile. It's the aerodynamic duo!

1.

2.

3.

4.

5.

6.

7.

8.

Full color prints of selected photographs, as indicated, are available from:

ATLANTIC FLYWAY, INC.
P.O. BOX 738
LAKEVILLE, CONNECTICUT
06039

Image size is 16" by 22" with an ample 1" border to accomodate trimming and custom framing. The overall 18" by 24" size will fit a standard frame. Extra heavy, glossy Vintage stock has been used to assure reproduction quality as close to the original photograph as possible. All prints are packed to assure their arriving in mint condition.

Send ($9.95) plus ($1.50) postage and handling. For each additional print ordered add ($1.00) postage and handling. New York and Connecticut residents please add appropriate sales tax.

The complete collection of 8 prints or any combination of 8 prints is available for a total price of ($65.00) plus ($3.50) postage and handling.

Additional copies of *George Meade's New York* may be ordered from Atlantic Flyway, Inc., for ($9.95) plus ($1.50) postage and handling.

79

All prices based on U.S. currency.